Stereo

(TYPE)

Stereo
(TYPE)

Jonah Mixon-Webster

Alfred A. Knopf New York 2021

THIS IS A BORZOI BOOK
PUBLISHED BY ALFRED A. KNOPF

Copyright © 2018, 2021 by Jonah Mixon-Webster

All rights reserved. Published in the United States by Alfred A. Knopf,
a division of Penguin Random House LLC, New York, and distributed in
Canada by Penguin Random House Canada Limited, Toronto. Originally
published in the United States in paperback, in slightly different form,
by Ahsahta Press, Boise, Idaho, in 2018.

www.aaknopf.com

Knopf, Borzoi Books, and the colophon are registered trademarks of
Penguin Random House LLC.

Library of Congress Cataloging-in-Publication Data
Names: Mixon-Webster, Jonah, [date] author.
Title: Stereo(type) / Jonah Mixon-Webster.
Description: New York : Alfred A. Knopf, 2021. | "This is a Borzoi Book" | Includes
bibliographical references.
Identifiers: LCCN 2020049987 | ISBN 9781524711948 (paperback) |
ISBN 9780593319369 (ebook)
Subjects: LCSH: Racism—Poetry. | Flint (Mich.)—History—Poetry. | Experimental
poetry. | LCGFT: Poetry.
Classification: LCC PS3613.I886 S74 2021 | DDC 811/.6—dc23
LC record available at https://lccn.loc.gov/2020049987

Cover design by John Gall

Manufactured in Canada
First Alfred A. Knopf Edition

To the UnCreatives, the Colonists

"Tell him not to preach so much rationalism and cold logic to these niggers. Let them alone. Let them sing curses at you in code and see your filth as simple lack of style. Don't make the mistake, through some irresponsible surge of Christian charity, of talking too much about the advantages of Western rationalism, or the great intellectual legacy of the white man, or maybe they'll begin to listen . . ."

—AMIRI BARAKA, *Dutchman*

Contents

Stereo
(TYPE)

Use this QR code to access digital works

Invocation of the Sacrosanct

Somatic Zombification Ritual for The Real Nigga with Resulting Poem

After William Wells Brown, Tisa Bryant, Glenda Carpio, Charles Chesnutt, Douglas Kearney, Adrian Piper, Richard Pryor, Ishmael Reed, Kara Walker, and Bert Williams

Instructions:

First. In a widely dark room, make the floor a circle of lit candles. Take a mirror big enough to fit a whole body and place it in the middle with you within. Leave enough space for movement. On repeat, play track 8, "Can I Live" from Jay-Z's *Reasonable Doubt* album.

Second. Find 6 stereotypical tokens of blackness for the body. An article for each: head, neck, wrists, ankles/feet (for mine's I chose a 59Fifty banged to the back, a Jesus piece, a Pelle Pelle with a fur collar, a (faux) platinum watch with the bracelet, and a pair of Timbs). Now accompany the tokens with 2 intoxicants—one to drink, one to inhale (for mine's I chose a fifth of Remy Martin and a Backwoods filled with some kill).

Third. In the middle of the circle, stand full bodied. Take whatever you have to sip on and pour some for the fallen. Next, take it to the head. Next, fire up. Next, fill your mouth with the names of niggas you know. Finally, in the mirror, practice your affectations for:

holla'n at yo' slime/homie/ock/patna/dunny/dude up the block (from tha heart): *"AYEEEE!!!!! WHAT'S GOOD MY NIGGA?!?!?"*

mimicking a gun-bust as you tell the story of the last nigga(s) you clapped (witcha' chest): *"DOO-DOOT-DOOT-DOOT!!!. . . . DOO-DOOT-DOOT!!!!"*

the song on the radio: *"Said dat I'ma ride fo' my muthafuckin' nigga | Most likely I'ma die wit my finga on the trigga | I been grindin' outside awl day wit my niggas | and I ain't goin' in 'less I'm wit my niggas | my nigga | my nigga"* **(say 3X's)**

the police: Mouth, fixed to say *"Maaann, I ain't even do shit!"* Hands, wherever the hell they tell you to put 'em. Make ass and balls part and lift ready.

a surprise: *"Maaann, swear fo' Gawd!!. .??"*

a conflict: Hands not up like "Don't shoot!!"— but out here like *"WHUTSUP?!?!?"*

Fourth. Leave. Turn up. Stunt. Flex. Turn up. Parkin' lot pimp. Ride down. Ride out. Turn up. Take note of how others interpret your actions and speech. Stop. Now. Write a poem that will raise you from the dead.

Song for the Unconscious Self; or First Freedom in Fo' Parts

"Cain't worry 'bout what anutha nigga think,
now that's liberation and baby I want it"
—Outkast, "Liberation"

Think: blank—meaning mirror-stage

makes a "nigga"
"real" meaning
here we are,
what we are, what
we still don't know

Think: apperception—as if black bodies are

victims of their own
psychic residuum—
say "nigga"
and try to remember
anything else

Think: blood—becoming the reflection

of a distant brother
you can tell y'all related
by how you mimic
his nostrils when pissed
or sobbing

Think: resistance—to occupy a wound

with a mouth
and ask,
"Now what 'nigga'
feel like having 'fun'
after that?!"

I

As well, we need to ask ourselves why the site of suffering so readily lends itself to inviting identification? Why is pain the conduit of identification?

—SAIDIYA HARTMAN, *Scenes of Subjection*

Black Martyrdom N° 6: *Litany of the Spectacle*

Come guillotine. Come gallows. Come gas soaked pyre. Come charred jaw. Come hot pike. Come hoary beast. Come ardent hunger. Come garrote wire. Come death wizard. Come adze. Come axe. Come taut rope. Come head knot, neck kink. Come click-clack. Come firing hammer. Come clank. Come bullet. Come wet smoke. Come slump body, bloody brook. Come bloated excision. Come slung wrist. Come wind rot. Come dead relic. Come unholy witness, onlooker lens. Come click, click, click, CLICK-CLACK-CLANK. Come bullet. Come bullet. Come bullet. Come bullet. Come bullet. Bullet. Bullet. Bullet. Bullet. Bullet. Bullet. Bullet. Bullet. Bullet. Bullet. Bullet. Bullet. Pull it. Pull it. Pull it. Pull it. Pull it. Pull it. Pull it. Pull it. Pull it. Pull it. Pull

Black Hauntology N° 5: Black *as if* always the blues

of a stridulated
half note—
night gristle,

locust chirp,
bowed neck,
wax lips, wet stain—

a body thronged
hard and buried
in the open light

the root of it
dug up with a mouth
stretched, reaching

to scratch the noose
from its throat
and give everyone a song

Black Hauntology Nº 6: *The Hang Around Blues*

ain't nun to do but hang around
ain't nun to do but hang around
and I ain't got no way
to make it out
tried to find me some help
know it can't be found

so ain't nun to do but hang around
ain't nuttin to do but hang around
ain't even got me a penny
to make a pound
they bout took all i had,
who am i now?

well ain't nun to do but hang around
ain't nun to do but hang out
if I could I'll run right
straight outta town
don't even need me no shoes
just feet on the ground

now ain't nun to do but hang around
ain't nun to do but hang around
ain't no new news
to think about
so I'ma tell you later
and I'ma tell you now

that ain't nun to do but hang around
ain't nun to do but hang around
now imagine if they never
woulda cut me down

say imagine if they never
woulda cut me down

I would have made it out (no question)
still be found
feet on the ground
outta town
could took a penny
and make a pound
out of water
and underground
said I tell you now
that I'd still be found
said I tell you now
that I'd still be found

Black Consumerism N° 0: *Tried Too Blues*

Said I tried to buy some freedom
but the price too high
my change too low
had to sell my brotha dreams
down at the sto'
oh why?
and it makes me cry

Said I tried to buy some love
but the price too high,
my change too low
had to sell my mama ring
down at the sto'
oh why?
y'know it makes me cry

Said I tried to buy some time
but the price too high,
my change too low
had to sell my daddy watch
down at the sto'
oh why?
and it makes me cry

Said I tried to buy some peace
but the price too high,
my change too low
had to sell my sister beauty
down at the sto'
oh why?
and it makes me cry

Said I tried to buy some hope
but the price too high,
my change too low
had to sell my uncle dope
down at the sto'
oh why?
and it makes me cry

Said I tried to buy some kindness
but the price too high,
my change too low
had to sell my auntie smile
down at the sto'
oh why?
and it makes me cry

Said I tried to buy attention
but the price too high,
my change too low
had to sell my cousin mind
down at the sto'
oh why?
and it makes me cry
y'know it makes me cry

Black Existentialism N° 12: *Da' Bad Nigga Blues*

always I wuz a nigga. *bad* at it. I wuz always bein' a nigga even when I wuzn't. I wuz a nigga, somebody's I wuz always bad at bein' even when I wuz a nigga I wuzn't. I wuz. bad at bein' a nigga tho' I wuzn't. I wuz bad at bein' a nigga even tho' I wuz a *real nigga,* or a *bad nigga,* or a *bitch nigga,* or a *fag nigga,* which I always wuz. always been bad, always a nigga. tho' I wuz bad at it I wuz *bad.* nigga, I wuz always a *bad nigga.* I wuz a *bad-bad nigga.* kept me a *hot nigga,* always nigga, always a nigga, it's always a *damn nigga,* always a nigga bad at it and always I wuz a nigga and always I wuz bad and bad and *bad* at it. really, I'm a *real nigga.* cuz all my niggas say I'm a *real nigga* and I bet if you go and ask my niggas, they gon all point at me and say *"NIGGA DAT'S A REAL NIGGA!!!"* really tho'— I'm bad at it. I am, really

Black Episteme N° 9: *This is what I know about blood*——

that when I wake in it,
my body turns the earth
with its gnashing. That when it appears
in my piss, all waters run silent.
That when I find it in my hands, I cannot
recall my name. Here, I offer you
a truism. I am not speaking of a cut,
nor the way my gut caves to touch
my back to some bullet, but
of what remains in the image of loss——
how it is signifier and referent at once,
how it pulls from my unending mouth.
How at this moment, I am sitting in a mess
of it, waiting for my own legs to stand——
how I could leave it
as a sign that still reads: *Nigger.*
You wasn't even here,

                    You wasn't even here at all.

In the Figurative, I Respond—*This shit be killing me!*

and these are the reports:

"Ol boy knocked the loaf of bread

out of dude hand up at Mini Mart,

they started arguing, and then ol boy left,

then came back

—shot off dude head like 12 times"

"Naw, cuz

ain't nobody sit pretty with that cuz"

"I wanna know who called

and told ol boy and nem

that dude was up at the sto'"

"It was all over like 4 zips

of some Chemdawg cuz"

"Right! Didn't I tell you that?"

"Look, I don't want them to do nothin'

to that boy mama, just to get to him—

cuz she my friend,

she do my nails and shit

I would hate it"

"They killed his lil sister the next day

at the park, shot four of 'em"

"Killed four of his people cuz

        killed his lil sister, his two lil kids,

 and his brother cuz"

                              "I aint hear about that"

"Yall ain't hear about that?"

                              "I thought that was connected"

"And blew that house up on Cherrylawn too cuz"

                              "Man they blew granny house

                    off the fuckin map"

"Shit ain't sweet round here cuz

        that's why you gotta be careful of who you touch"

                              "Cuz people got family

                      and shit"

        "It's ugly out here for y'all

        ██████"

                              "$100,000 wanted dead or alive"

"Yea cuz, that mean you can see his body

        right there cuz

                hangin'"

                              "$100,000?"

"The FBI, the ATF,
came to my mama house—
all of em—and said, *$100,000*
if you find him dead or alive"

"Bounty hunters, goons—"

"All of em?"

"Ain't you gon' tell
on that muthafucka?"

"Shit, hell yea!"

"Damn,
they got the hood and white folk
looking for the same nigga"

Black Hauntology Nº 10: *The Real Nigga in Dis Integration*

at this juncture,   inexorable meaning

through erasure,   in the signal of:

the edge, the   , the rib, the meat, the fat, the flesh, the coin, the silver, the blood, the juice, the box, the
     , the bird, the feather, the milk, the land, the bottle, the   , the lash, the nick, the dime, the dub,
the dust, the saw, the   , the shore, the shine, the shell, the man, the bull, the   , the   , the cup,
the air, the card, the sick, the   , the sheath, the shield, the   , the thief, the meal, the muscle,
the meat, the menace, the glass, the jaw, the weather, the wind, the salt, the wood, the word, the draw,
the   , the   , the skit, the skin, the   , the fit, the fitted, the   , the tassel, the tip, the
port, the stack, the stave, the dam, the deacon, the deck, the den, the   , the brain, the cave, the
star, the money, the   , the give, the   , the document, the   , the fact, the   , the scab, the
tap, the hen, the drain, the jowl, the   , the jest, the   , the stage, the track, the wine, the howl, the
     , the meter, the yolk, the   , the jam, the skull, the heft, the   , the   , the jut, the peek, the
fist, the jump, the   , the sea, the   , the   , the jip, the kin, the   , the kilt, the can, the ship,
the   , the shake, the kick, the chill, the string, the lake, the river, the mosh, the cap, the slit, the juke,
the   , the   , the breath, the bread, the break, the   , the chin, the tent, the bush, the   ,
the clutch, the lair, the   , the   , the   , the hush, the plea, the thrift, the   , the   , the
reed, the ring, the brass, the roach, the   , the foot, the gist, the shade, the scope, the   , the
mist, the   , the market, the matter, the   , the screw, the   , the lead, the ruger, the   ,
the mister, the mass, the clerk, the ticket, the   , the take, the shake, the bend, the gym, the case,
the   , the clip, the ex, the gin, the   , the fuse, the joust, the knife, the shit, the hum, the husk, the
comb, the   , the body, the stew, the strewn, the pitch, the throw, the   , the   , the push, the
meter, the mill, the grin, the tooth, the shun, the badge, the   , the   , the ball, the   , the sand,
the seat, the walk, the   , the gel, the   , the maker, the type, the light, the spell, the   , the
clean, the   , the post, the twitch, the bunker, the trench, the valley, the book, the   , the script, the
     , the   , the jacket, the church, the boy, the   , the stoop, the box, the sling, the laze, the
limb, the line, the axel, the tether, the limp, the stout, the   , the lame, the bag, the toast, the   ,
the   , the gill, the vicar, the   , the   , the   , the turn, the   , the cure, the code, the disc,
the   , the cook, the gene, the oil, the glue, the murk, the pot, the   , the score, the   , the shook

The Ghost of Richard Pryor Made Me Do It

Peoria, IL

Like any other night a white man sees me seeing him seeing me, I am again dead awake to the modes of awareness and it was as if him seeing me meant seeing me naked black, obviously black, ostensibly black, meant seeing me and you know what I mean already, I mean you know I was probably wearing something real black, like something blacker than black, something like a black hoodie with a black v-neck under it, a black snap back, black jeans, and black shoes and seeing me and seeing me in all of this meant he knew I was black, and I mean real black, naked black, obviously black, ostensibly black, and within proximity black still says *"Aye, gimmie a cigarette nigga"* to his white friend with me in earshot chose to say *"Yea nigga . . . I mean nigga . . . You know what I mean nigga . . . nigga . . . nigga-nigga-nigganiggganiggnigginignignanigga . . ."* to the extent I turn and while turning ask *"Why do you keep saying nigga so much?"* and I won't tell you what this white nigga said in response but it was the stupidest shit I've ever heard, I swear, and I won't repeat it, to which I tell him *"That's the stupidest shit I have ever heard, I think you need to stop saying that."* He says then, swiftly *"you can't tell me what to do nigga, nigga, nigga, nigga, nigga, c'mon nigga"* as if saying it meant seeing me meant seeing me naked black, obviously black, definitely black, unequivocally black and crazy enough to choke the language out his body and before I know it, my hand finds the back of this white nigga's shirt snatching it over into a cotton rope with the knot of a fist a noose I tighten with every giggle from the crowd.

Black Existentialism N° 13: *The Myth of Niggaphus*

Now here go this lil story bout this ol Greek nigga that all the mythologians try to keep tucked, but it's a few of us that still know the shit. Hell, them and some of them ol Renaissance artists also have you believin' there wunz't no niggas in ancient Greece—but it was a bunch of niggas in ancient Greece, and they wuzn't all slaves either. But anyway, now if you was ever into Greek mythology, then you know you got the gods, titans, nymphs, and the mortals and shit. Now this nigga Niggaphus was the darkest "mortal" anybody had ever seen in Greece. He was birthed as the orphaned son of Aphrodite—who always be starting shit—and some Ethiopian nigga that found his way to Troy. His folks found him when he was a little nigga, named him Niggaphus lowkey tryna be funny and shit—so now we all know what "Nigga" means, but "phus" comes from "phos" which is Greek meaning "light," feel me?

Now Niggaphus grew up to be the prototypical nigga: too black, too big, too fast, and too smart for his own damn good. The nigga won damn near every event in the first few Olympic games, he also was known to sneak off with anybody's somebody which altogether didn't sit too well with either the gods or the mortals. And so this one time he was tryna get to some booty—don't really know who from though. But anyhow, he had to cross this river to do it. So he was tryna cross this river, but the wind god Zephryus was hatin yet again, prolly becuz Niggaphus ain't want his ass neither. But anywho, so Zephryus sent this bad ass wind to knock Niggaphus off his boat and into the water knowing Niggaphus could do just about anything but swim. So that nigga pretty much drowned and shit. Now the other gods was still mad at him, for no reason really beyond the fact that he was too crafty a nigga, so they thought it would be hilarious and fitting to put him in Tartarus and punish the nigga by making him roll a big ass watermelon up a hill for all eternity and shit.

Now the gotcha was that every time Niggaphus got this big ass watermelon up the hill, it would just roll back down and he was gon' have to push it back up again. But what they didn't tell him was that this watermelon was gon' keep getting bigger and shit. So he'd been rolling this thing forth and back for who knows how long and shit, and the thing must have gotten to be bout as big as Tartarus itself. But Niggaphus wasn't no punk nigga, now, and all that watermelon rolling had made him even stronger than he was before. So one day he had got both fed up and hungry after turning this big ass watermelon to the hilltop one more time. And when the shit rolled back to the bottom, he went down and started to punch at the rind and shit. He kept punching til he put a crack in the side of it. Then he pulled it into halves and started eating away at the muhfucka, just going in on that shit. Slurping on the juice and shit. Bled the skin of its fruit and shit. The stunted little stems and shit. The label. And it ain't take him no time to eat it neither cuz the nigga was hungry. So he was all swole as hell after rollin and eatin' that huge ass melon, and he went over and slapped the dog shit out of Hades. Wuzn't nobody really tryna fuck with him after that, so he just walked straight out of Tartarus.

Now Niggaphus was hot I tell you and the only thing he could think of was putting them triflin' ass gods in they place, especially Zephryus. After leaving the caves and walking north, Niggaphus ran into Eros and snatched his ass up, demanding that he gave him entry to Mt. Olympus. Eros definitely ain't want no problems with Niggaphus either, so he obliged and helped guide Niggaphus to the ridge. After some travel, Eros and Niggaphus reached the home of the gods and the sight of him alone made all the gods tremble—bout shook the whole rock. But as soon as Niggaphus was getting ready to cuss they asses out, he started to gag. He held his gut but couldn't keep from spitting up the fruit. It all started coming out in one tide, and the force of all that watermelon spewing up his guts tore apart the corners of his mouth, ripping his body top down, then all at once and shit. Chunks of watermelon, blood, seeds, naps, and bowels laid flesh to flesh were thrown all over the temple. Zeus, disgusted by the sight, beckoned some shit called a tetramorph to lick the temple clean. The gods all basically agreed that the punishment did sorta backfire on them a lil bit, so the next time they used a rock instead.

Twitter Fingers

@A_ConceptualPoet/Artist/Whoever, After Gone with the Wind

Ooos Ise guessin yu kin stil be aneethin yu wan her missum!

gon hed an try oan da skin of som othas!

lak it duncha?

but yoos culdnta com up wid some otha beda contex
or consen or wat it is yal kine cals it? consep?

an ya say yoos wuz tryna sho or yoo wonnit
us ta see wut?

how dat otha wite wuman stil oan dem grinin skinin blak folks?

an yoo wonnit her asstate ta soo yoo?

dat wuz da hol punt rite?

den why is yoo stahp?!

gues ah berd in da han is stil werf mo den ten in da wuds
aint dat rite dere missum?

but cmon now missum, jus tween me and yoo
yoo did it causin yoo culd dednt ya?

one of dem red herrins dere ain ya?
yoo an missum Mahgret Mitcha

24

causin me and yoo bof kno gud an wel,
an wel maybe yoo do and wel maybe yoo don

an wel maybe yoo always new an jus ain kare,
dat yos lil tweets wuz all dun in wuts cald *fair yoose*

so we all kno dat meens thays cudnt eben soo yoo
iffin thays wonnit too!

but yoo ain meen ta offen nan cullad folks, rite?

by pasting sumbodee ded mammy an tryna fak her voise agin hun?

prolly guesin cullad folks ain hav nan feelins ta ofen hun?

guesin tha ownly thin yoo wuz outa mak wuz ah bad ideuh hun?

but yoo got people calin yoo and yoo calin yoself,
but yoo ain nan consepshul ahtis

yoo ain nan ahtis
yoo ain shit

And I'm Not All Nigger

for the Ancestors / after francine harris's "sift"

and I'm not all nigga

                          not all slung neck

                not all rope

      I'm not all broke back

                                not all pop pop

not all headshot nor jailbird

                    not all whistle at the white girl

I'm not all meat slump

                          not all cannon of teeth gliding cross

the Tallahatchie night-water

                    not all gun stipple and spilt blood

      not the boom of red smoke   breaking the body open

            with a new exit

            wet already

                    and I am not all body

      not all dead fruit dark swinging in the tree breeze

                          and though that is my blood,

I'm still not the blood on the leaves

                    still not all cotton   mouth

      hollow choke   hood-whip

                not all t-shirt slogan and hashtag   not all "Don't

shoot!!"

not all "I can't breathe!!"

                not some everlasting shadow of dead flesh

                    cuz even when I die,

      I'm still not all death

not all brown sugar stalk honey pot sour diesel

the blues and blue dream

naw— I'm not all nigga *boy*

I'm not all here   in this saying   not all is said

not the same haunt

and I come not as one   nor with nothing   still

I'm *still* and I still got my name—

I'm still Jennie

I'm still Laura   Still Lawrence

I'm still Emmett

I'm still Mike

I'm still Marie

I'm still Jerame

I'm still Tamir

I'm still Charley

I'm still Breonna

I'm still Freddie

I'm still Aiyanna

I'm still Eric

I'm still Rekia

I'm still Walter

I'm still Lavall

I'm still Sean

I'm still Korryn

I'm still Oscar

I'm still Trayvon

I'm still Amadou

I'm still Sandra

I'm still George

I'm still Elijah

I'm still Jordan   I'm still Tommy

and I'm still George

I'm still Daunte

I'm still Ma'Khia

I'm still Philando

I'm still Ahmaud

and my mama's still my mama

and my daddy's still my daddy

and my friends are still my friends

and these still all my brothas and sisters

and I still had my house

and my room

my garden and my job

and I still had my school

and I still graduated   remember?

I still had a life

before they took that

so when you tell my story,

get it right   and take

my shit back

II

Ashamed of what and naked before whom? Why let oneself be overcome with shame? And why this shame that blushes for being ashamed?

—JACQUES DERRIDA, *The Animal That Therefore I Am*

Psalm 6:6

and this is how a young nigga finds manhood |
at once constructed and crushed | into the body | on his back
drunk cheek to burnt floor | ass wet on fire and lifted toward the sky

of the den | a circling of wax-wood laths | the circle of his face
slopped shut | sodden | rugged scratch of skin | no sheath, but slick
not ghost, but gone | and the big homie thinks it is better like this | the mind of the boy

tucked in the black middle | his mouth muted in the liquid-smoke of his body
so even if, or when, he cums or wakes | there won't be such proof of the un/doing
beyond basement party on hush | beyond the hip's record of bent | beyond nothing

| not the hand cupped down on his neck | not the boxers lobbed| not the throat snuffed
| not the picture of one's mother on the wall watching | not the mother crying with her
boy crying | not the young paper-flesh ripped | not the bed he's made to swim in

Triptych in Which the Man Is Sometimes My Daddy

In the first dream:

The man runs past dropping a black feather. He stops. Turns back on his heel, leaning to pick it up. Places it inside of my front pocket. My hands do not complicate the matter. In me is a hard edge clapped with rain. What I am, he says, is the thing he wouldn't have. When I pull it out, I am a fallow child.

In the next dream:

The man runs past dropping a black feather. He is a crook and makes me swallow it. He opens his jean to the light until I bend. Until he is well-bricked inside the mouth that makes me. He swings my jaw with the bell of his hips. My head lies back into the knock. What is there causes me to look up, and I catch a dent of air in my chest. This is how I learn to say *water*.

In the other dream:

The feather is a headless bird and I am face down on a bathroom floor. Nothing is lit. The man's face bears the shadow. He takes me by the meat of my collar. Turns my ear over to say a quiet thing. In the next instance, he is the only one erect and the cutting opens a door in my gut. Aping what's already in two.

The Ugliest Nigga I Know / Is The Ugliest Nigga I Seen

In the half-shined picture refracted by the glass,
the sputtered window captures a negroid catalog:
back-neck black-black, a flag of naps, black
ear wax, black folliculitis, black
would-be empty holes in the eye, black
elbow and elbow, knees black capped, black
hand-bones like that nigga been diggin
coal barehanded, black patchy
crust from ringworm or another alien—
"Alligator skin" the brother says
before the fade, the brother's mama
yells *"Loose scalp!"* says, *"Yo' daddy*
got it too, y'all and them heads!"

        —once, a whole school bus full of 5th graders clapped and sang Parliament's
        "Flashlight" cuz light-skin Brittney said "his big fo' head" reflected the Sun
        like, obviously enough, a flashlight and that nigga ain't say a word

Self-Portrait in Stereotype Nº 1: *Negrohead Wif Nappy Hair*

On Juking with Another Black Boy

For Danez

When I walk towards you, I am an awkward thing. Up top too thick. Too lanky on bottom. Here I might wine too slow—or too fast. Forgive me if I give you my own beat to break to, if you smite me in the revel of sudden sweat, in the ghost of it coming off. Now. Let's call what our bodies do next a prompt. Do not pardon the grind, the almost fall. The almost fail of my thighs boomed heavy with laugh. There is a switch. There is music I can no longer name. There is an ache in my middle throat as I sang in false and you heard it. You hummed it too. Let the sound gape to land on my chest. Let its light flit in the moon-rush. At that moment, you call my arms a gate to any room, and I say our touching is the birth of some star we couldn't see

Ode to Darnell, the Erased Negro in the Middle of My Name

Darnell (English): 1. from Old French 'darnel', an annual grass, *Lolium temulentum*.
However, the plant was believed to produce intoxication.
2. Variant spelling of Darnall. A habitational name from
Old English *derne* 'hidden', 'secret' + *halh* 'nook'.
—*Dictionary of American Family Names*. Oxford University Press.

It was said,
"Heard melodies are sweet,
but those unheard are sweeter"
so in your name I listen not
for some nightingale to unhook
the chime from its would-be throat,
save for the whistle of a single flare
shot into the total blank
of the mind's expanse. From where
doth thou happy-light retain?
Upon what sweet and unsober face
lie furled the living shadow?
What swarthy grace doth soothe
your thirst for Sun?
O' darling gloom of muted horn
and firebush unsounding,
if thou were truly a plume of other earth,
I would pluck it from its steady dark
to keep for thyself only
etching endlessly, the hallowed
scores of thy name.

Self-Portrait in Stereotype N° 8:
Black as What Surrounds a Sickle Moon

> Here comes my tautology—
>
> *A blackness of a blackness of a blackness . . .*
>
> —Amaud Jamaul Johnson, "Pigmeat"

I.

you go on in the dark
wreath of midnight mornings
as dust nursed by twilight

I.

you mirror the cocked open neck
of a lost thing found in a plantation
forest, you and your shot-out eyes

I.

you and your swart eclipse
water stung by night rain
the pinpricked flag bent over it all

I.

a blank body born from a blank gut
the shadow-moth starved of day
its tongue hinged on its own wing

Cypher in Which I Cannot Save the Gangster Disciple in Boystown

For K

I imagine saying even your almost name would channel your body back from this night. Off the hip, we broke necks looking back from the curbs lipping onto the crosswalk staged for two men making eyes at the other. The time of any man's gaze is telling. And this too we talk, leaving our boys behind to procure a seat on the steps of anonymity. In front of a stranger's house you pull out and I do as you did. You tell me it gets fat. This too, a mirage you carry. And through skin we become neighbors. But naw, you are no *fag*. I call your name and your look is blank. You catch me stutter and step. You tell me you've made it. Tell me 26 in secret as if it were the winning number. As if with no logic you touch me like you could already. You say, *I used to be pretty*. Said, *man not no mo'*. And I want to sing it for you. About whatever and however you want. About the black tattoo tear-water. About the body you caught on this night. About the love for your niece you tell of in the passing minute. And I will do this thing trying to save you with my mouth. With its mirror of color and code. You ask if I know and I promise I know. You promise nothing. And what I do next is another defeat—write this, knowing it won't keep you.

Paranoiac Nº 3: *Prospicience*

is the ordinariness of color

is dirty money

is the last trap on the left

is the viscous part gone amok; an echo-shuffle of feet shucking

is the plug telling you he wouldn't bullshit

is the blackish rat he spit up——its body hobbled in bile, already a sung secret

is the phantom object

is getting juked out your last for what he said was *that loud*, but wasn't

is the dead wail of a red siren

is the way the houses bent the sound of it, breaking every light

is a wish sent to shield the body from vision

is one on each side and each side brightly beaming

is an obligatory curbside prayer

is a fever-dash of masquerade blooding up in thought

is soon glutted with the idea of rimfire, two shells, and a striking hammer

is a setup and I don't mind saying it

is a cop——or even a would-be hood nigga

is the shadow stare starting from the half-lit block

is when I knew they had it all planned out

is a Gestalt shift:

      a key, a flash of metal turned four-nickel already half-cocked

Paranoiac N° 5: *Hoplomania*

Everybody got a pistol | everybody got a .45
and the philosophy seems to be | at least as near as I can see
when other folks give up theirs | I'll give up mine
—Gil Scott-Heron, "Gun"

The gun appears at a gathering of little niggas in the driveway. The gun appears with a pearl handle, in silk, in a lockbox inside my mother's headboard. The gun appears on the belt of a middle school liaison. The gun appears in leather atop my father's woven-wood placemat. The gun appears tucked on the waist of my big brother. The gun appears with those other niggas at the Mini Mart. The gun appears as a shotty pointed before my windshield. The gun appears in the bando on the bend of its cushion. The gun appears in chrome, stuck through the window of a Dodge, firing outside of Paradise. The gun appears as signage. The gun appears soaking the lot with a steady light. The gun appears behind the bulletproof glass at BP. The gun appears in hand at the table of a drunk. The gun appears as a misfire. The gun appears at my boy's crib—as a stick. The gun appears before the weather. The gun appears unbuckled on the officers who abound me. The gun appears in the basement, a father and his three sons fill thirty clips that hold fifteen rounds each. The gun appears in double. The gun appears on a strap while my other brother eats a sandwich. The gun appears on the counter behind where I sit. The gun appears in the mind of my Uber driver having heard me make a clink. The gun appears loaded. The gun appears as a Warhol—a print tacked on the head of a shut room. The gun appears off another hip. The gun appears in front of the tiny air in my face. The gun appears as a joke. The gun appears as my fist in a hot mouth in no time.

The Real Nigga Mimics His Right Hand

and why else would a nigga's hands be this ashy?
the only ritual I keep is hustle—first near-dead skin
sent searing cross unhinged crackle crushed
nail hung from nob and gnawed thumb
-chaff, finally, now the day is through—
and this is how I know I put in *work*.
A word every nigga know the business of.
Bread, double fisted in a hand dry with picking
wall from the corner of a room. The body's ruin,
a milked pebble at every hour. You know
dusty knuckles is a good hunch
say *pocket money*
say *back rent*
say *a chicken in the pot*
say
say
say
say   lookit baws,   na
my hans jus as wite is yose!

III

Fixity, as the sign of cultural/historical/racial difference in the discourse of colonialism, is a paradoxical mode of representation: it connotes rigidity and an unchanging order as well as disorder, degeneracy and daemonic repetition. Likewise the stereotype, which is its major discursive strategy, is a form of knowledge and identification that vacillates between what is always 'in place', already known, and something that must be anxiously repeated . . .

—HOMI BHABBA, *The Location of Culture*

Black Existentialism N° 8: *Ad Infinitum; or Ad Nauseam*

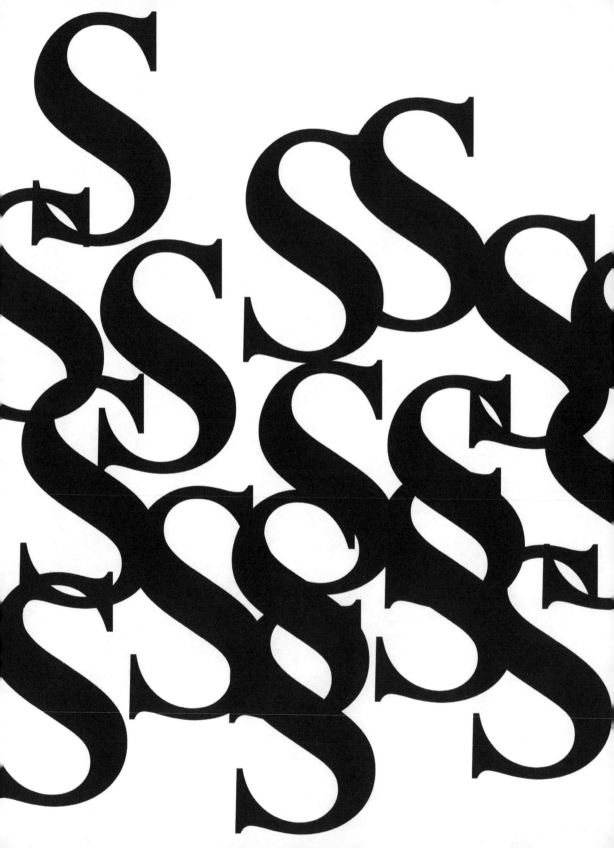

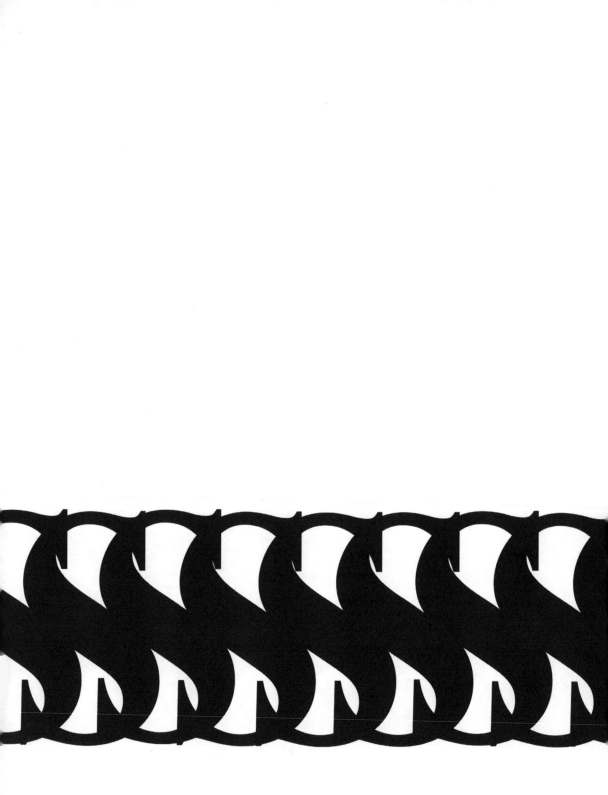

IV

"If you were going to put something in a population to keep them down for generations to come — it would be lead."

—DR. MONA HANNA-ATTISHA

"I am sorry. And I will fix it."

—GOVERNOR RICK SNYDER

Based on Actual Events /
Attempts to Survive the Apocalypse

Prologue

On April 25th, 2014, the City of Flint, MI—now a postindustrial site of contamination—had its water supply changed from the Detroit-provided Lake Huron water to the Flint River. Residents of Flint, MI, have long reported a foul stench coming from the river waters below the Linden Road Bridge on the city's north-west side for an indefinite amount of time. The smell of rot, always. Concurrently, the Flint media outlets, city officials, and citizens have reported multiple findings of dead bodies within and near the Flint River. Yet, authorities—emergency managers Edward Kurtz (2012–2013) and Darnell Earley (2013–2015)—both appointed by Governor Rick Snyder—ensured the use of the Flint River for the source of the city's main water supply as a rescission to the city's budget. However, the Flint Water Plant was not thoroughly equipped to filter out the harmful pollutants and residents began voicing concerns regarding the water's noxious smell, murky yellowish-brown color, foul tastes, and innumerable ailments listed as but not limited to: rashes, boils, loss of hair, seizures, pneumonia and pneumonia-like symptoms, irritable bowels, and vomiting. During this time, coliform bacteria including Escherichia coli was detected in the water supply. Chlorine was added to the water to remedy the damage in response.

In October 2014, General Motors discontinued its use of the Flint tap citing that the water was corroding their car parts. General Motors then swiftly switched its source back to the Detroit/Lake Huron line. Despite outcries throughout the city, Mayor Dane Walling assured residents that the water was safe to drink. Between the years 2014 and 2015, an outbreak of Legionnaires disease spiked in the city. Ninety cases (and counting) have been reported, along with 12 fatalities. In addition to the polluted water, Flint residents discovered the city was a testing site for military "urban warfare" drills from June 2nd through June 10th, 2015. An uprising began in the city that ultimately spurred a more conclusive investigation generated by a dedicated pack of Flint residents including Nayyirah Shariff, Melissa Mays, LeeAnne Walters, and Claire McClinton. In August 2015 Dr. Mona

Hanna-Attisha (a scientist and pediatrician at Flint's Hurly Hospital) and Marc Edwards (a civil engineer) went public with research that would confirm the presence of lead in the drinking water and lead poisoning in the children of Flint. Preventive corrosion methods were never utilized by the Flint Water Plant, though it is a well-known fact that chlorine is a corrosive agent.

The abrasive chemical wore away at the pipes and began releasing lead into the water supply. Speaking of the effects of lead poisoning, Dr. Hanna-Attisha states, "Lead is a potent known neurotoxin. The CDC, the AAP, everybody tells us that there is no safe level of lead . . . your cognition and behavior, it actually drops your I.Q." The "2015 Annual Water Quality Report" remitted by the City of Flint also affirmed the findings of chemical by-products in the form of total trihalomethanes (a carcinogenic compound) during the testing period of January 1st to October 16th 2015. The City of Flint incurred Safe Drinking Water Act violations due to its high trihalomethane levels. The cause of this presence has been linked to chlorine having a chemical reaction with organic matter such as plant material, natural pollutants, and decay. Through various local media, the City of Flint issued and withdrew multiple boil water notices. But still, studies show that boiling water does not eradicate nor prevent the production of other disinfection by-products. According to the CDC, boiling water is actually shown to increase the concentrations of lead. In December 2015 the recently elected Mayor of Flint, Karen Weaver, declared a State of Emergency and Governor Rick Snyder followed suit in January 2016 after growing pressures from his constituency. The Michigan National Guard was deployed to assist with water distribution.

On May 4th, 2016, the 44th U.S. President, Barack Obama, made a visit to Flint Northwestern High School to pull a stunt—he fielded complaint narratives, took one sip of clear water, and left, only to return to the city in 2020 to campaign for Joe Biden and to shoot a three-pointer from long range. Through the remainder of 2016, multiple government officials who were implicated in the Flint Water Crisis were charged with various counts including involuntary manslaughter and conspiracy. Yet, most of the defendants were able to reach plea deals in which no jail time was served. After a federal judge orders mandatory door-to-door water delivery to homes whose lead service lines had not been switched, citizens began reporting that some water deliveries were actually a ruse to serve warrants on targeted individuals. Activist Melissa Mays warns that police would knock on a person's door claiming to deliver water but would present a warrant for someone's arrest and take them to be prosecuted. In February 2017, Richard Baird announces that the Flint water bill subsidy would soon expire and this was doubled-down upon in May when 8,000 Flint residents received notices that their water services would be shut off due to non-payment. The State of Michigan sued the City of Flint that following June, stating that the city was endangering the public by not entering into a contract with the Great Lakes Water Authority. Yet, in their October 2017 report, the Environmental Protection Agency concludes that the Michigan Department of Environmental Quality was comprehensively responsible for Flint's failed water infrastructure. Amidst the blame shifting, residents were alerted by the State that water donations were coming to an end and distribution centers would close before Summer 2018. It is reported that approximately 23,000 service lines were checked, and 9,000 lead pipelines were replaced by mid-2019.

On June 3rd, 2019, authorities confiscated the mobile devices and other documents possessed by State officials as part of an ongoing Flint Water Crisis investigation. However, 10 days later, State of Michigan Attorney General Dana Nessel announced that all charges against the remaining officials in the Flint Water Crisis would be formally dismissed in support of the decisions of Solicitor General Fadwa Hammoud and Wayne County Prosecutor Kym L. Worthy, who cited negligence on the part of the previous lead investigator Todd Flood. In an attempt to assuage the community in her announcement Attorney General Dana Nessel stated, "I want to remind the people of Flint that justice delayed is not always justice denied." A study from the Michigan Department of Education shows an increase in Flint special education needs students by 56 percent between the years 2013 and 2019. Near the end of 2019, it was announced that a new juvenile detention complex would be built to replace the Genesee Valley Regional Center. Of the plans for the new build, Judge John Gadola commented, "What you are going to see in two years is Genesee County go from using portions of a 100-year-old facility to [being on] the cutting edge and putting Genesee County at the forefront of juvenile justice." Residents of Flint have begun a sustained protest against these plans, believing that officials want to construct a different pipeline, one that funnels their children from school to prison.

As lead pipe replacement and the repair of neighborhood roads, sidewalks, and lawns continued well into 2020, the global COVID-19 pandemic and statewide quarantine ordinances added to Flint citizens' struggles with accessing economic and day-to-day resources. During the height of the COVID-19 pandemic, Flint and the surrounding Genesee County suffered additional deaths and other compounding public health risks that exceed those experienced in 16 states across the country. In August of 2020, the State of Michigan announced a $600 million settlement with the residents of the city, with the majority of funds going to the children that were harmed as a result of the Flint Water Crisis. The City of Flint incurred an additional Safe Drinking Water act violation for failing to test enough homes for copper and lead during the earlier half of the year. The newly elected Mayor Sheldon Neeley attributes this violation to residents being resistant to city personnel entering their homes.

In January 2021, nine people were indicted for their negligence in the Flint Water Crisis including former emergency manager Darnell Early who faces up to five years in prison for misconduct in office and former Governor Rick Snyder who faces one year for willful neglect of duty. Other charges range from petty misdemeanors to felony involuntary manslaughter. After multiple failed attempts to charge those responsible, Flint citizens remain skeptical of prosecutors' hope to secure convictions. As of February 2021, lead pipes are still being removed throughout various neighborhoods—a failure to meet the November 30th, 2020 deadline set by an agreement with the Natural Resources Defense Council and the December 31st, 2020 deadline for State funding. Multiple residences and other sites throughout the city continue to display an unusual color or odor to their water with other notable effects on skin, hair, and clothing. While some samples throughout the city reveal the presence of lead in the water, some homes and businesses test below the federal action level (15 parts per billion) and their water source remains treated with only a filter. Today, Flint citizens continue resisting the crisis through advocacy and action groups, counternarratives, and organizing their own water and food drives to defend their families from terrors both invisible and inevitable.

Breach

March 25th 2014—A water main has broken at an unspecified location. August 16th, 2014—Tests confirm the presence of fecal coliform bacteria in the tap water on Flint's west side. A "Boil Water Advisory" has been put into effect. September 5th, 2014—Tests confirm the presence of fecal coliform bacteria affecting the water in all directions. A "Boil Water Advisory" has been put into effect. September 6th, 2014—Tests confirm the presence of fecal coliform bacteria affecting the water in all directions. A "Boil Water Advisory" has been put into effect. January 2nd, 2015—A water main has broken at an unspecified location. January 7th, 2015—A water main has broken at an unspecified location. February 3rd, 2015—A water main has broken at an unspecified location. February 5th, 2015—A water main has broken at an unspecified location. February 6th, 2015—A water main has broken at an unspecified location. April 11th, 2015—A water main has broken at an unspecified location. June 15th, 2015—A water main has broken at an unspecified location. September 2nd, 2015—A water main has broken at an unspecified location. February 9th, 2016—A water main has broken near Dort Highway affecting the water in all directions. A "Boil Water Advisory" has been put into effect. March 5th, 2017—A water main has broken at an unspecified location. March 9th, 2017—A water main has broken at an unspecified location. April 11th, 2017—A water main has broken at an unspecified location. May 14th, 2017—A water main has broken at an unspecified location. June 15th, 2017—A water main has broken at an unspecified location. March 5th, 2018—A water main has broken at an unspecified location. June 15th, 2018—A water main has broken at an unspecified location. June 23rd, 2018—A water main has broken at an unspecified location. September 2nd, 2018—A water main has broken at an unspecified location. March 9th, 2019—A water main has broken at an unspecified location. June 15th, 2019—A water main has broken at an unspecified location. June 23rd, 2019—A water main has broken at an unspecified location. September 15th, 2019—A water main has broken at an unspecified location. February 5th, 2020—A water main has broken at an unspecified location. February 6th, 2020—A water main has broken near City Hall affecting the water in all directions. A "Boil Water Advisory" has been put into effect. February 9th, 2020—A water main has broken at an unspecified location. September 2nd, 2020—A water main has broken at an unspecified location. A "Boil Water Advisory" has been put into effect.

Incubation

It is 2020 and the City of Flint Says,
"Don't boil the water"

And I refuse to drink a single drop
from any tap or bottle now. I've stopped
bathing completely, waiting for rain to slick
my skin back on. I eat accessory fruits
mainly from cardboard and cover
the rashes on my face with coconut oil
to appear more alive—I sit beneath a sunlamp
touching no one.

It is 2016 and the City of Flint says,
"Boil the water"

My mother lays her head in a couch of her own hair,
pulls back a scar from the watermark in her leg,
the scalp of her knee giving to the bloody lock—
Faucet water hardens into a fang, attacks,
slowly un-fleshes the body altogether.

This week, my niece goes live on Facebook
filming her son running in an errant stupor.
"Bad" as he is already, vaulting up
an obstacle of leather, a base
from which to rehearse flight.

He lands, runs
onto the carpet, the screech following
his shade into the mat.
He moves his joints to the finish—
muscle where his mind angles the floor.

It is 2014 and the City of Flint says,
"Boil the water"

My niece, great-nephew, and I
bowl metallic mac and cheese
from the aluminum. We all smash it
heavy and wet the taste
in the soup of our mouth.
TJ plays the last noodle
with his finger, consumes it—
says, *"Where the meat?"*

It is 2017 and the City of Flint says,
"Boil the water"

I undo the gauze from the stitched together
incision below my navel. The procedure:
an embolization to loosen the knot
of veins growing inside me.

And to clean the wound,
I use a room temperature bottle
of purified drinking water, more gauze,
and a plain bar of antibacterial soap.

I apply a small amount of Bactine
to the area and stick on
a hospital grade bandage. I press
onto it lightly for ten seconds.

It is 2014 and the City of Flint says,
"Don't boil the water"

I lie into a nightmare of sound. Again,
there is no rest. The whole house

and hood is washed in the voice
of some agent installed in the part-
burned projects adjacent to the crib, tucked
in the half of a half of an acre, an *alarm*,
a holler on blast every night
from 10 pm until we all sleep it off.

This lasts for a year, despite complaint.
Another day starts like this, stretched by the mile
of voice sounding from the intersection
of Pierson and Cloverlawn, throwing itself
to the undead which lay some distance elsewhere—
the broke record of it   in the air   in the water
in dream: !!!WARNING!!!

!!!WARNING!!!

!!!YOU HAVE VIOLATED AN AREA PROTECTED BY SECURITY!!!

!!!THE AUTHORITIES HAVE BEEN NOTIFIED!!!

!!!LEAVE IMMEDIATELY!!!

!!!WARNING!!!

!!!WARNING!!!

!!!YOU HAVE VIOLATED AN AREA PROTECTED BY SECURITY!!!

!!!THE AUTHORITIES HAVE BEEN NOTIFIED!!!

!!!LEAVE IMMEDIATELY!!!

!!!WARNING!!!

!!!WARNING!!!

!!!YOU HAVE VIOLATED AN AREA PROTECTED BY SECURITY!!!

!!!THE AUTHORITIES HAVE BEEN NOTIFIED!!!

!!!WARNING!!!

!!!LEAVE IMMEDIATELY!!!

!!!WARNING!!!

!!!YOU HAVE VIOLATED AN AREA PROTECTED BY SECURITY!!!

!!!THE AUTHORITIES HAVE BEEN NOTIFIED!!!

!!!LEAVE IMMEDIATELY!!!

!!!WARNING!!!

!!!WARNING!!!

!!!YOU HAVE VIOLATED AN AREA PROTECTED BY SECURITY!!!

!!!THE AUTHORITIES HAVE BEEN NOTIFIED!!!

!!!LEAVE IMMEDIATELY!!!

!!!WARNING!!!

!!!WARNING!!!

!!!YOU HAVE VIOLATED AN AREA PROTECTED BY SECURITY!!!

!!!WARNING!!!

!!!THE AUTHORITIES HAVE BEEN NOTIFIED!!!

!!!WARNING!!!

!!!LEAVE IMMEDIATELY!!!

!!!YOU HAVE VIOLATED AN AREA PROTECTED BY SECURITY!!!

!!!WARNING!!!

!!!THE AUTHORITIES HAVE BEEN NOTIFIED!!!

!!!WARNING!!!

!!!LEAVE IMMEDIATELY!!!

!!!YOU HAVE VIOLATED AN AREA PROTECTED BY SECURITY!!!

!!!THE AUTHORITIES HAVE BEEN NOTIFIED BY SECURITY!!!

!!!WARNING!!!

!!!LEAVE IMMEDIATELY!!!

!!!THE AUTHORITIES HAVE BEEN NOTIFIED!!!

!!!LEAVE IMMEDIATELY!!!

!!!WARNING!!!

!!!YOU HAVE VIOLATED AN AREA PROTECTED

BY SECURITY!!!

!!!THE AUTHORITIES HAVE BEEN NOT

!!!LEAVE IMMEDIATELY!!!

!!!WARNING!!!

!!!WARNING!!!

!!!WARNING!!!

!!!YOU HAVE VIOLATED YOU HAVE VIOLATED AN AREA PR

!!!THE AUTHORITIES HAVE BEEN NOTIFIED!!! BY SECURITY!!!

!!!LEAVE IMMEDIATELY!!!

!!!THE AUTHORITIES HAVE BEEN NO

!!!LEAVE IMMEDIATELY!!! !!

!!!WARNING!!!

!!!WARNING!!!

!!!THE AUTHORITIES HAVE BEEN NOTIFIED!!!

!!!LEAVE IMMEDIATELY!!!

!!!LEAVE IMMEDIATELY!!!

!!!LEAVE!!!

It is 2015 and the City of Flint says,
"Boil the water"

I return to the city for the first time
since the story surfaced. Riding through the hood,
crossing at the corner of Pierson and Dupont,
stands a string of neon stanchions,
military servicemen, a gaggle of palettes,
a gaggle of bottled waters wishing us well.

It is 2018 and the City of Flint says,
"Don't boil the water"

Soon, a new narrative: *lead exposed* as opposed to
lead poisoned. The spin of an incident as accident,
a posture to say, *I guess we all were just a little naïve.*
As counter to, *Yes. We did this with our full knowing.*
Education and training, notwithstanding—
surely, you can trust us now?

It is 2020 and the City of Flint says,
"Boil the water"

Bills, flyers, pamphlets, bags, bills, manuals,
mailers, bills, boxes, bills, bottles, bottle caps,
bills, a junk flood in the streets
overflowing our houses now. Every piece
of litter and literature yelling—
consume, consume.

It is 2019 and the voice on the radio says,
"Have you or your family been affected
by the Flint Water Crisis? Does your child's blood
levels show evidence of lead poisoning? Have you noticed

any rashes or developmental issues in your child? If so,
you maybe eligible to file a claim and receive
compensation for you and your child's suffering.
Please call us at the law offices of . . . "

It is 2015 and the City of Flint says,
"Boil the water"

My boy Q posts a picture of his back
bubbling with fissures in an even spread—
having bathed in the city's northeast waters,
the contagion carries itself into the host,
bearing witness to a feast of skin
and other soft metals.

Recovered_Conversation _0105.wav

Friday April 4th, 2014 8:55 PM
In a trap house off Pierson Rd
(names have been redacted to protect the ill-informed)
The sound file can be accessed here:

█████ : We is walkin' dead around here, █████ . . . Least you get the chance to go back, to you know, Ypsilanti and shit and see people who bright and sunny.

███ : Yea . . .

███ : But right here, if you just sitting here . . .

███ : It's the walkin' dead.

███ : It's gon' get closer and closer. Niggas gon' keep dying. Next thing you know, it's gon' be a nigga you see every damn day. And that nigga gon'.

█████ : It's the walkin' dead . . . It's the walkin' dead around here.

███ : Got you pissed off.

█████ : Niggas, I swear to God on everything I love, niggas is zombies around Flint. It's the walkin' dead . . . I swear it's the walkin' dead around this bitch.

████ : The younger the niggas is, the more bullshit.

█████ : I remember the time when you was so young, that everybody just had a job because it was Flint, and all the jobs was here. Now everybody—you can't even get a job in this bitch, so all you doin' is getting' fucked up and doin' what you—

███ : Niggas tryna get a job. You know them little programs, you go to Mott. Niggas tryna get a job, but shiddd, at least they was goin' for it, getting that permit, that work permit. If you was 14, you got that permit.

█████ : It's the walkin' dead around here. It was never how it was when we was coming up. Even in our teens, it was still kinda lenient to where [inaudible] muhfuckas. But in

85

these last, since like 2010, it's been the walkin' dead. On some real shit since like 2008, but since 2010, it ain't been nothin' but the walkin' dead. And ever since you talked to me like I just wanna do whatever I gotta do to bring this bitch up off my back, you know what I'm saying? Ever since you told that shit to me ███, like I feel you, cuz that's some real shit. That's how you should be coming from this damn dungeon, but it's like it wasn't a dungeon when we was young, it was more like a cave, when we were *young*. Like, you still was able to get out and get what you needed to get, but you couldn't get what you wanted to get. But now it's like a dungeon, you can't get what you need or you want. You know what I'm sayin'? It's really hard. And that's why I'm like I wish I really listened to my granny, cuz my granny was really givin' us the game man. That's one thing, my granny was really givin us the game. Wouldn't grasp it. We wouldn't listen to her. Be like "Aw she old, she don't know what she talkin bout. I don't give a fuck how many syrup and pills you sold, you can't tell me shit!" I swear, we wouldn't listen to her old ass, we thought she was old and we thought she was crazy. On some real shit. And even then I was like "I don't think you crazy and shit," but I be like "this bitch crazy." Man my granny was givin' us the game, and I wouldn't take it.

███: I was just confused as hell.

Frequently Asked Questions

It is 2016 and the State of Michigan says:

Why do I have to boil my water?

A "Boil Water Advisory" has been issued by the City of Flint due to a drop in pressure in the City of Flint water supply. Due to this drop in pressure, bacterial contamination may have occurred in the water system. Bacteria are not generally harmful and are common throughout our environment. Corrective measures are currently underway to remedy the situation.

Should I use bottled water?

Water from an alternative water source is the best option during a "Boil Water Advisory." When bottled water is available, it is a good alternative to boiling water.

What is the proper way to disinfect my water so it is safe to drink or prepare other drinks like baby bottles, drink mixes, tea, frozen juices, etc.?

The best method of treatment for those served by the City of Flint Water department is to first filter the water through an NSF-approved water filter. Then, the water must be boiled. Boiling water kills harmful bacteria and parasites (freezing will not disinfect water). Bring water to a full rolling boil for at least 1 minute to kill most infectious organisms (germs). For areas without power, disinfect tap water by adding 8 drops, about 1/8 teaspoon, of plain unscented household bleach to a gallon of water. Thoroughly mix the solution and allow the water to stand for 30 minutes.

Can I just use my filter instead of boiling water?

No. You must boil the water after you run it through the filter during the "Boil Water Advisory."

Can I use tap water to brush my teeth?

No. Do not use tap water to brush your teeth. Use bottled water or water that has been filtered and boiled or disinfected as you would for drinking.

How should I wash my hands during a boil water advisory?

Vigorous handwashing with soap and your tap water is safe for basic personal hygiene. However, if you are washing your hands to prepare food, you should use boiled (then cooled) water, disinfected or bottled water with handwashing soap.

Is potentially contaminated water safe for bathing and shaving?

The water may be used for showering, baths, shaving and washing, if absolutely necessary, but don't swallow water or allow it to get in your eyes, nose or mouth. Children and disabled individuals should have their bath supervised to make sure water is not ingested. Minimize bathing time. Though the risk of illness is minimal, individuals who have recent surgical wounds, have compromised immune systems, or have a chronic illness may want to consider using bottled or boiled water for cleansing until the advisory is lifted.

How should I wash fruit, vegetables, and food preparation surfaces or make ice?

Wash fruit and vegetables with filtered and boiled (then cooled water) or bottled water or water sanitized with 8 drops (about 1/8 teaspoon) of unscented household bleach per gallon of filtered water. Also, use filtered and boiled water to wash surfaces where food is prepared. Ice should be made with filtered and boiled water, bottled water or disinfected water.

What do I do with food and drink prepared during the advisory?

Throw away uncooked food, beverages or ice cubes if made or prepared using tap water during the day of the advisory.

How does a "Boil Water Advisory" affect feeding my infant?

Mothers who are breastfeeding should continue to breastfeed their babies. Wash and sterilize all baby bottles and nipples before each use. If this is not possible, then single-serve, ready to feed bottles of formula must be used with a sterilized nipple. Always filter and boil water before mixing concentrated liquid or powdered formula. If unable to boil filtered water, water may be disinfected as described for drinking.

What if I have already consumed potentially contaminated water?

Even if someone has consumed potentially contaminated water before they were aware of the boil water advisory, the likelihood of becoming ill is low. Anyone experiencing symptoms such as diarrhea, nausea, vomiting, abdominal cramps, with or without fever, should contact their healthcare provider. Symptoms associated with waterborne illness are also associated with food-borne illness, or even the common cold.

What infectious organisms might be present in contaminated water?

Illnesses from contaminated water occur principally by ingesting water. The major organisms that produce illnesses are protozoa such as Giardia and Cryptosporidium, and bacteria, such as Shigella, E. coli, and viruses. These organisms primarily affect the gastrointestinal system, causing diarrhea, abdominal cramps, nausea, and vomiting with or without fever. Most of these illnesses are not usually serious or life-threatening except in the elderly, the very young or those with compromised immune systems.

What happens after the boil water advisory has ended?

You will be notified by the City of Flint when the boil water advisory has been lifted. Once the boil advisory has been lifted, you must change the cartridge in your water filter. The water filter can then be used with the new cartridge.

Where can I get additional information?

www.cdc.gov

Other Frequently Asked Questions

It is 2020 and the Environmental Protection Agency says:

Is it safe for adults to shower or bathe with Flint water? Can babies be bathed in tap water?

Yes. Your skin does not absorb lead in water. If plain tap water has too much lead, bathing and showering is still safe for children and adults. It is safe even if the skin has minor cuts or scrapes. Never drink bathwater, and do not allow babies and children to drink bathwater. Rashes have many causes, but no medical link between rashes and unfiltered water has been found. If you have concerns, call your primary care doctor and call 2-1-1.

Is it safe to wash dishes and do laundry with unfiltered water?

Yes, but dry them after. Wash dishes, bottles, and toys with unfiltered soapy water. Dry before use. Lead in water will not be absorbed by porcelain, metal, or glass. Clothes washed in plain tap water will not contain enough lead to cause harm.

Will water contaminated with lead hurt me or my children?

Lead exposure can affect nearly every system in the body. It may not have obvious symptoms, so people might not realize they have too much lead in their bodies. For young children, exposure to lead can cause behavior problems and learning disabilities. The only way to know if you have lead in your body is to get tested.

We (residents) have been getting information on how to use water safely from many different organizations, and sometimes that information is conflicting. Who should we listen to?

EPA is coordinating with the City, State, and other federal agencies to respond to all of the issues with Flint's water. Until further notice, EPA advises that residents should always use a water filter.

Will EPA change any of its policies based on what happened in Flint?

EPA is actively considering potential revisions to the Lead and Copper Rule. The primary goal is to improve the effectiveness of the Rule in reducing exposure to lead and copper from drinking water. EPA anticipates proposed rule changes will be published in 2017. In the more immediate future, EPA will be issuing clarifications on how samples should be collected based on concerns raised by Flint residents and others.

How long will EPA's response team be in Flint?

EPA will be here as long as it takes to make sure the water is safe to drink. EPA's recent order also requires the city to provide the appropriate level of staffing and training to ensure that the water plant and distribution system can be effectively operated and maintained.

The filters being handed out by the City are only rated to filter out 150 ppb (parts per billion) or lower of lead. Many have lead results higher than that. Does that mean the filters are not working?

EPA continues to recommend that Flint residents use NSF-certified filters in their homes to remove lead. EPA's latest sampling results confirm that these filters are effective in removing lead from drinking water, even at higher levels.

Will whole house filters or reverse-osmosis filters be offered to residents?

A whole-home filter may not be effective because it does not treat water that flows through interior pipes, brass, and leaded-solder, which can contaminate the water with lead even after it has passed through a whole-home filter. Any water treatment filter used should be NSF-53 certified to remove lead and should be located at the end of the plumbing right before the tap, so that all water that flows through home plumbing is treated.

Black-on-Black Stone / Under a White Stone

After César Vallejo

I will die in Flint, in the early gloaming of a raid

     as blood honeys the fetid water.

I will die in Flint, in a handoff without witness

     on any night. Perhaps, *this* night

I am found with broadcloth over my teeth,

     a bagged object in clutch, empty

water bottles at my side, a dingy hoard of glooms,

     and whatever's left of my body

now enters the day rearward. In some nature,

     Jonah Mixon-Webster is dead

and weaponless. A fortuitous echo sucking air out,

     a shrunk-mouthed portal shrilling

its sole evidence of event—

     a darkening, then all at once, snow.

July 25th, 2018

Excursus: *A Reverie*

Light tricks itself from the rim of my sleep // a drink hangs my head through the gap of a thin bottle // as if for no ordinary reason, two black birds collapse into the hem of this horizon // now the sudden weight of it // the thresh of my belly, blunt puckered in the sun // with no hum nor cloud do I come to you // O' object of your too-soon body // O' muscle of my timely end // if I had more in me, I would leave this thing here //   // the image that must cleave in its want // the weapon fully naked // in one lop, I would scissor off the part bit by the ill horse // in the house of no wave—in the breach // my hair is comely still, and made for a man's fist // the man knuckles a sea of feathers // gives to the fleshy knot // my bullnuts // my loose scalp // when it is over, we do not tarry in our language // the quiet flings itself like a basehead // on my back, the memory is kept on a thread I pull to speak // that is an attempt to lose the man you know is everywhere // this is an attempt at a volta—two niggas chase each other through a hedgerow where no one can find // now neither one is it

Acknowledgments

First and foremost, all gratitude to the High Spirit, angels, and ancestors who shared their presences in this work.

Thank you to the City of Flint and everyone in it for showing the world what resistance looks like.

Thank you to my parents Carolyn J. Mixon and Moses W. Webster for their unconditional love and support of my attempts in this life. Thank you to all of my family for your rooting for and sharing with me, my granny Pecolia; my auntie team: Helen, Beatrice, Evelyn, Christa, Rosemary, Eunita, Sharon, and Nikita. My sisters and brothers Saundra, Mary, Demetrius, Derrick, LaDarris, Denairio, Reese, Darnell; and chosen fam TaCee Boaz, Nabila Lovelace, Derrick Harriell, Gabriel Gudding, Airea D. Matthews, Ricardo Cortez Cruz, Justin Phillip Reed, Gabriel Ramirez, L. Lamar Wilson, Ladan Osman, and my Ypsi fam Carla Harryman, Christine Hume, Rob Halpern, Christine Neufeld, Jeff Clark. Very special thank you to Danny Boy Steward and Angie Fisher for sharing their gifts with this project.

All gratitude to the jurors of the Windham-Campbell Prize for changing the lives of my family and my work.

Very special thank you to my agent Julia Eagleton for being so supportive, even from the U.K.; my editor Tim O'Connell for being so open, believing, and dedicated to *Stereo(TYPE)*, and for having fun with me in this process. This was some true serendipity.

Thank you to everyone at the Knopf/Penguin Random House editorial, art, production, publicity, and marketing staff for all the beautiful and innovative ideas and care you all brought to this project: Rob Shapiro, Eenie Bernard, Matthew Sciarappa, and all others whose name I may not have known, thank you.

And to you reading this, thank you for taking the time and energy reading and listening to this project.

Nothing but gratitude.

A Note About the Author

JONAH MIXON-WEBSTER is a poet-educator, scholar, and conceptual/sound artist from Flint, Michigan. *Stereo(TYPE)*, his debut poetry collection, received the 2019 PEN America/Joyce Osterweil Award and was a finalist for the 2019 Lambda Literary Award for Gay Poetry. He is an alumnus of Eastern Michigan University and received a Ph.D. in English/Creative Writing from Illinois State University. He is the recipient of the Windham-Campbell Prize for Poetry and his work is featured in various publications including *Harper's Magazine, The Yale Review, Jazz & Culture, Callaloo, Pennsound, Best New Poets 2017,* and *Best American Experimental Writing 2018.*

A Note on the Type

The text of this book was composed in Apollo, the first typeface ever originated specifically for film composition. Designed by Adrian Frutiger and issued by the Monotype Corporation of London in 1964, Apollo is not only a versatile typeface suitable for many uses but also pleasant to read in all of its sizes.

Printed and bound by Friesens, Altona, Manitoba